THE SAILOR'S EDGE

Published in the United States by Holt, Rinehart and
Winston, 383 Madison Avenue, New York, New York 10017.

Published simultaneously in Canada by Holt, Rinehart and
Winston of Canada, Limited.

LIBRARY OF CONGRESS CATALOGING IN PUBLICATION DATA

Forster, Daniel.
    The sailor's edge.

        1.   Sailing.   2.   Sailboat racing.   3.   Windsurfing.
4.   Sailboats.   I.   Broze, Jay.   II.   Title.
GV811.F65   1985   797.1'24   85-14130
ISBN 0-03-006057-5

First American Edition.
Produced and designed by Les Ateliers du Nord, Lausanne,
Switzerland.

Printed in Switzerland.

10 9 8 7 6 5 4 3 2 1

PUBLISHER'S NOTE

THE SAILOR'S EDGE is divided in four parts, representing the competitive characteristics of each racing style. To afford maximum visual impact, Daniel Forster's photographs are unburdened by words. Instead captions identifying the boats, skippers and races are included in a photographic index at the back of this book.

ACKNOWLEDGMENTS

To my parents for their encouragement when I was starting out and to my wife Christine who found the missing puzzle pieces during the realization of this book and who is always waiting on shore for me.

I would especially like to thank: Jean-François Genoud for having approached me with the idea to do this book; René Leonarduzzi and Jack Macrae for believing in our project; Toni Lutz for telling me in 1971 to show my photographs to the Swiss magazine YACHTING; Bill Robinson for giving me the first opportunity to publish my work in the United States; Keith Taylor of SAIL magazine for his commitment to my work; Jay Broze, Francesca Lodigiani and Jörg Neupert who did the interviews with impossible deadlines; Keith Beken for taking me out in his boat and Stanley Rosenfeld for giving me film when I was desperate; all my boat drivers, who do an essential part of my work.

Daniel Forster
August 1985

THE SAIL

OR'S   EDGE

Photographs by Daniel Forster
Text by Jay Broze

Holt, Rinehart and Winston
New York

I met Daniel Forster at Newport during the 1977 America's Cup trials. All I knew about Daniel (Dahn-yell, emphasis on the second syllable) was that he was originally Swiss (before becoming a citizen of the international sailing fraternity), was a photographer, and that he had taken "my" seat aboard the Goodyear blimp. Later it became common knowledge that he had finished second in the Society of International Nautical Scribes (S.I.N.S.) yodelling contest; there had been only one entrant. In the ensuing years of working with and around Daniel, I have come to appreciate his remarkable talents. He puns in three or four languages, he is almost universally well regarded within a sailing community where egos are rampant, and he is greeted warmly by maxi-boat owners and windsurfers alike. Also, if there is a gracious hostess with a house overlooking the harbor, then Daniel and his wife Christine are probably dining there tonight. Best of all, Daniel Forster takes superb photographs, and despite his best laid plans, they are photographs of boats and sailors.

Daniel Forster had but one firm resolve when he apprenticed to a studio photographer in Bern. He did not want to become a yachting photographer. Forster is an avid sailor, as his former master/employer, Toni Lutz. "On Monday we would talk about yesterday's race, and on Friday we'd talk about tomorrow's. In between we talked photography, and I was quite convinced that it was more fun to sail than take pictures." Daniel's work has since taken him to three America's Cups, seven Admiral's Cups, four Olympic games, fifteen Kiel Week regattas, and three times around the globe chasing windsurfers. I think he could count the days spent sailing, strictly for pleasure, on his fingers.

His loss has been our gain, for in the last fourteen years Daniel has become the most sought after sailing photographer in the world. The fact that he began his career in 1971 using borrowed equipment ("In the studio we had no SLR cameras"), that he included a case of mistaken identity in his first assignement, ("At Kiel they thought that I was the editor of Swiss magazine YACHTING"), and that sea-sickness reduced him to shooting through a portlight ("I spent my first offshore race in the starboard berth") only adds to the irony of a Swiss photographer, who proudly claims to be "centrally located in the countryside" reaching such prominence in his profession. His recipe for success seems deceptively simple.

Daniel admits that he has been the regular beneficiary of changes within his craft and his sport. Added to that good fortune are an unusually steady hand, some solid technical training in the studio, and a willingness to work just a little harder than most of his contemporaries. In the early days he survived by servicing the myriad of small sailing magazines in Western Europe. He says "I still carry a map of Europe in my head…" with little magazines in each country around Switzerland, each one needing a slightly different kind of picture." At the 1972 Olympics in Kiel, Daniel sold pictures he developed overnight to any editor who looked interested. He took advantage of the first of the plastic printing papers released in Europe to do "about ten time as many glossy prints as I could have done a year before." He also purchased his own cameras for the Olympics, Canons, that he claimed were superior to the Nikons of that era. He sold his Finn class dinghy to raise the funds for those cameras.

1972 was a false start for Daniel. After an accounting of the checks generated by all that hustle and bustle in Switzerland, France, England and Germany, he saw that there was a very meager living to be made selling boat pictures, even when you wrote German and French race reports to go along with them. So Daniel went back to a Geneva studio and photographed watches, "watchmakers are the worst people in the world to shoot pictures as they are used to working in micro-millimeters, and your work, your whole attitude, has to match their way of looking at things." Of course the watchmakers paid quite a bit better than small sailing magazines, but within a year the choice was clear, "either make more money and have three weeks vacation a year, or make very little money and travel to where the boats are." The boats won, and Daniel took his show on the road from regatta to regatta, hawking his wares.

Photo editors, first European and later American, quickly realized that Daniel was taking more than his cameras to these events. He had a new way of looking at the things he photographed. One art director said he "stacked images," another editor called it "lip reading photography." They could all spot "the Forster spinnaker shot." In Daniel's own words, "I have always tried to find the decisive moment of action. As a sailor I keep looking for the moment when the man on the bow, or the dinghy sailor, has to make his decision, has to make his move. So I always found a person at the center of the picture." And, always, he's alert to the sailor's edge, the smart move that separates a winning helmsman from the rest of the fleet.

Technical advances in lenses made this kind of action stalking easier than it had been in the past. With lighter and brighter lenses, all photographers were able to bring the action closer, but Daniel says he noticed an odd thing on the press boats. "I saw that I was often using a lens one size longer than the rest of the photographers. Or sometimes I would be shooting at a 250th of a second, while everyone else was shooting at a 500th." Daniel has a steady hand, and to hear him tell it, he always has. Little boys in Switzerland compete in crossbow archery, shades of William Tell, and Daniel did well. In the Swiss army, which everyone joins, he did equally well with the rifle. Whether the crossbow made him steady, or his steadiness made him good with the bow, is anyone's guess, but the results with the camera were immediately noticeable to art directors at sailing magazines. The combination of sailing experience, equipment, and a hand, made his pictures something very special in the mid Seventies.

"Style" is almost unconscious in sports photography. People shoot that which they can sell, and editors grow used to buying what is shot. Stanley Rosenfeld, the dean of American sailing photographers, was brought up in a photographer's family, and his family archives are a repository of east coast yachting history. His family style evolved from the kind of portrait photographs possible at the turn of the century. Beautiful forms, the shapes of light and shadow, the texture of water, fog, and sky, and above all the boat, dominate the composition of Stanley's pictures. After World War II, he was able to use 35 mm equipment to capture what he likes to call the "emotion" of the picture, and the smaller gear allowed him to work more quickly at establishing form, line, and drama. Stanley has said that when it became possible to capture the action with the new equipment, considerations such as the unity of a crew's body language was a major factor in deciding whether a photo was shot or released for publication.

The overall statement of Stanley's work is one of dynamic power and elegance. Other American photographers took the Rosenfeld look as their ideal, and chased it through new locales, new shooting platforms (notably the helicopter), and new subjects. In 1975, the vast majority of photographs in American magazines could be called Rosenfeldian. In England one could make a similar statement about the Beken family of photographers.

Daniel Forster, the Swiss small-boat sailor, had no such tradition. Even today he admits that he misses at least half of his shots because he is waiting to see what the people in the pictures are about to do. "I think I identify too much with the sailors. I know that they have to release the afterguy, or do a roll-tack, so I hesitate, waiting for the move, and too often the picture goes by." The photographs that don't escape usually look as though they were trying, too. Boats are about ram the viewer, spinnakers are vanishing before your eyes, spray is flying, sailors are staring into the camera, wondering what is coming next. People seem to pop up out of nowhere in the photos, and in place of unity of body language you often see comedians. In the place of dynamic force one often gets chaos. There is an anarchy of boats, sails and people in many of Daniel's photos, and that anarchy caught the eyes of the photo editors. The ability to appreciate the anarchy, and to see the composition of a great picture through it, is what Daniel thinks of as his edge over most other picture takers.

Stanley Rosenfeld has said that in a great sailing photograph there should be no "dead spots," places were the eye is drawn, only to be abandoned with nothing to look at. Daniel's version of this outlook holds that there ought to be something more on the page than just a sailing picture. "People should get to look more than once at a picture. The great boat portraits have been done, all we can do there is make new versions for the new boats. Or we can make pictures that deserve a second look." The photograph of KIALOA rounding one of the Channel Forts is this kind of picture. We learn almost as much about the boat from it's being masked by the rectangular silhouette of the fort as we would from a classic owner's shot. The two gulls flying in formation above the tower are worth many second looks. Do they mirror the boat, or does the boat mirror them?

Daniel believes that most of his shots are documentary, "I have to show the people how this place is different from some other one, the color of the water, the skies, the shoreline, and the kind of boats that are there." The photos have to stand along side all the others in any number of magazines, and Daniel thinks the documentary quality, "green water and thunderstorms instead of crystal water and volcanoes" sets them apart. It also makes it easier for Daniel to sort his work back in the office. There, he has files for the Olympics and Olympic classes, for calendar and cover shots, offshore racers, sunsets, clouds, waves, Twelve Meter yachts, maxi-boats, and VIPs. Then there are all the windsurfer subcategories. "I have a good memory for time and place, and when some client wants a certain kind of picture I can probably match their layout and color choices." All it takes is a couple of years in a studio learning how to make the most out of every hour.

Daniel's recipe for successful sailing pictures isn't really so simple afterall. An aspiring shooter needs very good equipment, long bright lenses, an instant appreciation of what is about to happen, the ability to read sea states and boat motion, an infallible eye for form, line, tension, and movement, and the skills to compose these things in the viewfinder, with the right exposure, shutter speed, and film. Also, the camera can't jiggle. Compared to this, writing about sailing is a snap. Unfortunately, this is only part of it.

"Almost half the problem in taking good sailing pictures is finding a good photo boat and a driver who knows about sailing," says Daniel, and most of his contemporaries would agree. The bitterest stories within the craft revolve around broken down boats and idiot drivers. Even the gentlest souls have longed to bludgeon uncooperative boatmen to the decks with their telephoto lenses. A good photoboat will take you right into the action, and out again before you are run down, blocked out, or foul the very subject you are trying to shoot. For efficiency's sake, you should arrive just in time for the first race, "you have to know what day the racing actually starts, and not show up till then. All the tune up days for a World's Championship just cost you money." Confidants claim that the only time Daniel was ever early to an event was in Kingston, for the 1976 Olympics. That was excusable, since he was hitchhiking from New York to Canada, sleeping on boats and in the bushes of freeway medians, "It was my first trip to America and I wanted an adventure."

A serious sailing photographer also has to be philosophical. "The worst moment is when you are reloading and all you can hear are the motordrives of the other guys, zing, zing, zing, zing." Sometimes you hire the helicopter for the day there is no wind, and take the inflatable motorboat when it's blowing forty knots. Sometimes the cameras malfunction, sometimes they sink.

Daniel lost his first set of Canons when he and a friend, François Perrin, crash broached a centerboard lake cruiser. "We were running down the lake, and the Joran wind coming down off the Jura mountains was building up. We finally realized that we had better get the spinnaker down, so I sent my friend forward. Of course the bow went right underwater, and I was left steering air with the rudder. Whoops, over we went, and one complete set of cameras and lenses went to the bottom of Lake Neuchâtel." At the other end of the scale, was the disaster of the VELSHEDA, the restored J-boat pictured in the Prestige section. Daniel went forward as the vessel ghosted past the slips. He was shooting back down the deck as she reached for the open sea. Soon only the very bow was dry as spray sheeted over the foredeck, then things got serious. Once in open water she displayed the seakeeping qualities that made 130-foot J-boats so much like U-boats, and punched right through the waves. Daniel scrambled up the headstay as his feet washed out from under him. By the time a crewman crawled forward with a safety line, water was running in and out of the camera bodies. "But they were insured, the worst was that one of my New Balance deck shoes had been swept off my foot, and they had just stopped making them. The skipper was not sympathetic."

Most skippers are sympathetic, however. In today's sailing community every sailloft wants pictures, every owner wants to be immortalized, every designer wants his boats on the magazine covers, and every hand wants to see himself in a magazine or a book. All these wants provide work for Daniel Forster and his fellow photographers, and they provide a window right into the racers cockpit for all the armchair sailors, weekend cruisers, and perpetual boat varnishers among us. So put down the paint brush, and put up your feet, and see what other sailors have been doing for Daniel Forster all these years. These are the images that he has chosen from thousands in the files: the ones that explain why he is out there every week with his cameras.

A C R O

B   A   T   I   C

"There are two ways to photograph wavejumping. You can put on a wetsuit, take out your waterproof cameras and be bashed around in the surf for an hour or so. Or you sit on the beach with your tripod and long long lens and figure that you will have a more patient eye than the thirty other photographers on the beach with you."

As the photos in this section show, Daniel has a remarkable eye, wet or dry. His pictures also reveal the amazing changes in methods of boardsailing during the past decade.

Boardsailing is an example of a great idea that never went far at home in California. Hoyle Schweitzer and Jim Drake came up with the "modern" sailboard in the late Sixties and a friend suggested they call it a "Windsurfer". In the heady atmosphere of 1970 California, windsurfing looked like a natural winner, but it barely made a dent. Surfers are as conservative as archbishops, beach sailors were already happy crashing through the waves in catamarans and dinghy racers didn't see any advantage in standing up. At best some yachtsmen considered sailboards only an interesting novelty, something like a sea-going skateboard and occasionally windsurfers could be seen strapped to the lifelines of cruising boats. There were some few true believers, but there seemed to be no niche for the sailboard in American watersports. For Schweitzer and his dealers the windsurfer was an exercise in marketing frustration.

When the first sailboards arrived in Europe they met with immediate success and the sport grew geometrically from day one. European sailing is far more class oriented than in America and far more expensive, relative to the level of personal income. The sailboard gave thousands of people a way to get on the water cheaply, tens of thousands followed, then hundreds of thousands. Sailing became much like skiing, all a person needed was a rack on top of the Fiat and he could bypass the stodgy yacht clubs, the incredibly expensive moorage fees and the social conventions that went along with "yachting".

Manufacturers in every western European country began pumping out boards and sails, some were superb, some were terrible and almost all were immediately slapped with patent violation suits from Schweitzer's Windsurfer Corporation. The legal battles barely made a ripple in the European boardsailing community, however, and the world champions in all kinds of class associations came from Holland, Italy, Germany, Norway and France. Rivers, lakes and bays were covered with people hanging onto multicolored sails, standing on white boards, sailing around triangular race courses. Experimental classes were devised, strict development formulas were written and young boardsailors studied the racing rules as carefully as any Laser skipper in the United States. For European sailboard designers and manufacturers the future was in racing, in regattas and in attaining Olympic status. On the other side of the world, however, something entirely different was evolving.

In the Hawaiian Islands, blessed with sunshine, beaches and tradewinds, boardsailors actually had a surf to go along with their wind. While racing back and forth through the breakers, they discovered that the speed of the wave coming into the beach, combined with the speed of the outbound board could launch an intrepid sailor like a rocket. Board shapes and hardware began a rapid evolution as everyone who had the spare time tried his or her hand at making a board fly better. On the Baltic people were trying to sail into the wind, at Diamond Head one could try to soar into it. Kailua on Oahu, Hookipa on Maui and later Torquay in Australia became meccas, and as Daniel puts it, "Suddenly no one wanted pictures of traditional races anymore. They wanted waves, waves, waves." The gray Baltic was dead, the blue Pacific was alive.

Wavejumping is a photographic carnival. The practitioners fly, soar, crash and crumple. There is a lovely streak of madness running right through the endeavor. Daffy Duck wouldn't try such inverted flight and mothers around the world began to warn their children to stay out of the surf. At times the jumpers combine the most amazing aspects of dirtbike riding and space walking and all the while the rollers thunder into the beach all around them. Anyone who thinks wavejumping is somehow the lazy way out of the discipline of "really racing", hasn't been sanded down by one of these mountains moving in on the beach.

The young men and women who are the best are athletic, usually handsome and suntanned; often famous everywhere but America. The top rank of the world's board-sailors is currently heavily weighted towards Hawaii. When the rules shifted to wave-jumping, to long triangles, to ocean endurance races and to "slaloms" in and out through the surf, the people who had lived with waves and surf all their lives gained an immediate advantage. Robby Naish is arguably the absolute best, but Alex Aguera, Peter Cabrinha, Matt Schweitzer, Cort Larned and the rest who are close behind him at the top, are simply better at this than anyone could imagine.

A   T   H   L

T

E T I C

T

There is a tremendous competitive allure to one-design racing. The boats are as identical as they can be, crews are similar in weight and stature and the thickness of one's wallet is of little consequence on the race course. If you win one-designs, you can realistically call yourself the best sailor in that class on that day. If you lose, there are few egosalving excuses. The Olympic classes in this section offer all of that and more. This is where the best are bred and medal winners in this arena will show up at the wheels of every kind of racing boat imaginable.

This is Daniel Forster's kind of racing and Kiel Week is his favorite race meeting. There are dozens of tricks and illusions in these photos, as racers appear to hover without boats, or sail seems to fit any number of hulls in its vicinity. It is hard not to feel the water rushing by your chair as you look at many of these pictures. The boats and sailors have been captured, almost indecently exposed, in moments of total concentration. Some moments are grand, others catastrophic, but there are no pretensions of elegance, only much effort and much bravado.

The Olympic classes have no monopoly on this single-mindedness. An Etchells championship, the Laser nationals, or a 505 Worlds will show as much tension and intent and many of the sailors in these photos have won titles in other one-design classes. The difference in an Olympic regatta is that all the boats are on the water at once. From the air the number of classes and courses looks like chaos, from the water there is an incredible variety of action. One of the big problems is deciding what to shoot, particularly in hard fought meetings where three or four class medals may depend on the outcome of the final races. Also, the mood of the photographer plays a part. Is it going to be a day for sprinting through the spray alongside the catamarans, or for watching the ballet of the Solings? Will he shoot the loneliness of Finn sailors, or the teamwork of the Flying Dutchmen?

"Every class has a style, a personality," according to Daniel Forster. "To capture the Finn style, you need to show who is the boss at the outset. The winning sailor first controls the boat alone, and then controls the race course." It's not easy to accomplish, but John Bertrand's intent demeanor offers an important clue to his winning style.

"The 470 sailors are the wild ones, on and off the race course. They start the food fights; their races result in general recalls, occasionally they even crash into each other. Clearly, it's a class of chaos." The 470 is a collegiate boat in the United States, a youth class around the world. This fact, combined with the class limit on crew weight, makes for high-spirited hyper-active sailors.

In contrast, the Flying Dutchman is a very powerful dinghy that requires a big crew to keep it upright and precise control to keep it in contention. The fine tuners with strong arms do very well, but those who let the boats get away do very badly, like the unfortunate skipper climbing out of his boat at the jibe mark as the competition flies by.

"Catamarans are like airplanes flying above the water. They cut through waves then crash down into the ocean. The skippers must try to be pilots." The speed differential between seemingly identical Tornado cats can be astouding and they are made to seem insignificant by the differences in acceleration. The boats are designed to fly, not to tack and getting up to speed first is the crucial requirement for victory. Tornadoes are usually considered young men's boats, but Poul Elvström (who used to be referred to as "God" by other dinghy sailors) and his daughter prove his contention that "a boat is a boat is a boat," no matter what it looks like.

The Star is one of the oldest surviving racing machines. It began as a gaff-rigger and its remarkable evolution has kept it in the forefront of hardware development for decades. For fiddlers and fussers, it is a boat made in heaven; innovators and boat-speed fanatics have a history of success in the class. Lowell North, perhaps the king of the "let's see if it works" community, has multiple medals and championships in the Star and Dennis Conner, who institutionalized the methodical search for perfection, was a standout World Champion in the class. But it is more than a fast boat; tenacious decision making and pure sailing ability put Buddy Melges and Tom Blackaller at the top of the class as well. "The Star sailor always looks like he is waiting for the mast to fall down on him. He is sailing the rig, trying to keep that thin little stick up there. They always appear surprised after a jibe on a windy day, like they expected the mainsail to carry the rig away."

The Soling is a team boat. No skipper ever carried a weak crew to a medal in Solings and often it is hard to tell who is really in charge. All three men move as one in the tacks and each one has a crucial job as the boat goes round. Usually the bow man calls tactics, the middle man trims and the skipper tries to find the way through the waves. The three men behind the wave in one of Daniel's pictures represent about as much talent as could ever be placed on one small boat. As a trio they are on their way to the gold medal.

P   O   W   E

R F U L

IT

Daniel Forster will readily admit that having a good photo boat to shoot from and a skipper who knows about sailing is an essential part of the battle for great sailing photographs. The validity of this statement is most obvious in the following section. The S.O.R.C. (Southern Ocean Racing Conference), Admiral's Cup, Clipper Cup, Sardinia Cup and the Southern Cross Series are big free-form race meetings, with the minimum of controls and a maximum of congestion. The boats range from big and expensive to very big and very expensive. They offer spectacular photo opportunities if you can get close enough to the right boat at the right place, at the right time. These events attract every sailing photographer on the host continent and the difference between being published and being run over is your skill in getting the camera platform in exactly the right place.

These boats and these events are the epitome of what many in the Olympic classes call "checkbook" racing. The International Offshore Rule is a development formula that encourages owners and designers to spend time and money coming up with new boats. If some are too fast, too light, or too outlandish, then the Rule will change and everyone starts all over again. For the price of a high-technology 40 footer with a full inventory of sails, a skipper could campaign a one-design boat for the entire four year Olympic cycle. Board manufacturers spend less per year on their entire official teams than these owners spend on one boat. The expense of developing and building big I.O.R. racers rises each year like the costly fighterplanes, since no one can be sure just what the crucial advantage might be and where it will be found, everything must be tried.

The size of the bank accounts in these fleets guarantees that there will be plenty of professionals on hand to assist in the spending decisions. This is the realm of what used to be called the "factory team". Now everyone in the top echelon sails with some combination of the following formula: a guest "rock star" from the sailmaker, a person from the spar company, a sailor/engineer from the builder to keep track of the stresses and strains, perhaps a young and athletic member of the designer's staff, often a salesman or technician from the instrument and computer supplier, plus assorted favorite companions. Though venues change as the year passes, many of the same faces appear on the Isle of Wight and the Island of Oahu. All the regattas pictured in this section attract the manufacturers maintenance staffs, ready to remove and replace or repair any piece of gear that may fail. The parking lots from Sydney to Sardinia will be littered with vans bearing boat logos along their sides and service trucks from the major saillofts. This league is often called Grand Prix racing, not because the quality of sailing is any better than in the Olympic classes, but because it replicates so exactly the travelling circus atmosphere of auto racing.

The S.O.R.C. is the hardest of these regattas to photograph. It began as a winter meeting for the northern sailors and it trails around Florida from St. Petersburg to Nassau, with races on both coasts and two overnighters in between. Also, the organizers can still remember the days when the S.O.R.C. was a "gentleman's" event, without all the professionalism and media attention, so they were often deaf to the needs of photographers until CIBA agreed to sponsor a press facility. Daniel comments, "you often spend two and a half weeks with nothing, then get your magic day in the Bahamas. Still, you can't risk not being on hand for the whole thing."

You can usually spot a S.O.R.C. photo by the color of the water, but the Admiral's Cup, off Cowes on the Isle of Wight, is noted for its skies, or lack of them. Still hanging on to the title of world's premier team racing meet, the Admiral's Cup is typified by huge fleets (part of Cowes week), big tides, strong currents, flukey winds, English food and deadly-serious national teams. The outcome is often decided by the concluding race to Fastnet light and back and more than one favorite has ended his campaign stuck on a shingle bar or a mudbank after misjudging the state of the tide and current.

The Clipper Cup and the Hawaiian Islands are the platonic opposites of the Admiral's Cup and England. Tradewinds and tradewinds' skies, teams primarily from the Pacific Rim, no tides at all and the chance to tan yourself to your heart's content are the stuff of Clipper Cup. Also, a skipper has the option of shredding his spinnakers, dropping his mast over the side and tearing his boat apart. These are not lake conditions and heavy-air teams from Australia and New Zealand are always respectable here.

The Sardinia Cup is the only one of the five events in this group that did not grow out of some local regatta. Like all of the Costa Smeralda it is the creation of the Aga Khan and its entry list is limited to three boat national teams. Light hazy days alternate with clear mistrals and whether you are winning or losing, the food is excellent, the coffee is strong and the spectators are very rich.

The Southern Cross Series in Sydney, Australia, is a holiday extravaganza, combining Christmas, New Year and southern hemisphere high summer. It too has huge crowds on the water, faithful winds and a classic ocean race as its finale. The Sydney to Hobart race is probably the most predictably windy "wrap up" race in the world. At the S.O.R.C. the gulfstream sea conditions in the St. Petersburg to Fort Lauderdale race can be gruesome in a cold winter northerly, the Round the State race in Hawaii has two tough legs and sudden winds can make Fastnet surprising and dangerous, while the race across Bass Straits, between Australia and Tasmania, is almost always hard sailing. The 1985 edition, in fact, saw two thirds of the fleet withdraw.

The portrait of ZERO is taken off "the organ pipes" on Tasmania. This is a pure Daniel Forster "documentary" portrait. Is the boat highlighting the cliffs, or are the cliffs the backdrop for the boat?

S.O.R.C.

Admiral's Cup

Clipper Cup

Sardinia Cup

Southern Cross Series

PREST

T

IGIOUS

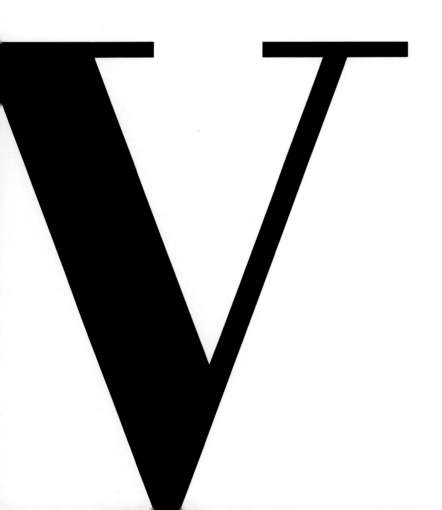

No yacht can ever recapture the power and drive that strained the rigs of clipper ships, but the vessels in this section come as close as any ever will. By the time a racing yacht grows to eighty feet, with her rig up well over a hundred, she is ready to break records. Clipper ships for all their romance, hauled cargo and their pyramids of canvas, were built to move tea, gold and wool. A racing boat built to the maximum size of the current racing rule, is a faster machine. The fastest elapsed time for a sailing circumnavigation of the world was recorded by a yacht racing for the Whitbread trophy. As this book goes to press, half a dozen of these "maxi" boats are setting out to break that record.

The maximum raters that are today racing around the world are actually an aberration in the evolution of the breed. Most of the big boats have been built to campaign in a maxi circuit, a travelling circus that relegates them to the role of day racers. As day racers, the big I.O.R. boats are following in the footsteps of the J-boats like VELSHEDA, becoming superb high-technology exotics, the toys of very rich men. The boats racing round the world are financed by corporate sponsors, the ones racing round the buoys are financed by their owners. These men don't have the time to race across oceans, so they rendez-vous with their yachts and their crews at pleasant ports of call, such as Honolulu, Sardinia, San Francisco, Newport, Las Palmas, the south of England in the summer, Southern California or Florida in winter. In these locales they sail out to race their giants as though they were dinghies.

Some maxi owners, especially KIALOA's Jim Kilroy, are consumed by big-boat racing, constantly modifying and improving the existing boat, and always shopping for the next one. These yachts are immensely expensive (a new 80 footer, all up on the starting line will cost between one and two million dollars) and have a limited resale value, so it is not unusual for an owner, like Kilroy, or Bob Bell of CONDOR, or Huey Long of ONDINE to be saddled with a new and old edition at the same time. The crews of these giants are gypsies, travelling with the boats, or meeting them at each port of call, filling the spaces between the Olympic medal winners, sailmakers, esteemed tacticians and America's Cup veterans who are always included among the two dozen hands on board. Professionals in every way but income, the "fillers" of the most serious maxis include large numbers of New Zealanders and Australians seeking to make the contact that will set them up with the "real" professionals in the saillofts or boatbuilding yards.

At the St. Francis series in San Francisco Bay, the last event on the Maxis' 1984 schedule, Jim Kilroy and the crew of KIALOA struggled mightily to keep up with the superior BOOMERANG. On one medium-air day Kilroy, Dennis Conner and crew managed to ace the start and stay ahead for the entire race. When they got the shifts, they lengthened the lead; when BOOMERANG closed, Conner proved to be impossible to pass. Still, there was no question that in winning four or five races BOOMERANG was convincingly better than the rest of her class. Jungle Jim's response to KIALOA's new status on the track was, "we are looking at a couple of alternatives that the crew and I have generated and talking with some designers who we think will be able to give us the numbers we think we should have." A spokesman from "the crew" translated that to, "we haven't chosen the designer, but the next KIALOA will be a serious racing boat."

Herbert von Karajan of HELISARA typifies another kind of owner. For some Europeans the maxi-boat is just another stylish prop, one that goes along with the family jet, the house in St. Moritz and a stable of race horses. For these skippers there are only two or three events in the year, the week at St. Tropez, a week in Sardinia and perhaps the Middle Sea Race, or the Aegean Rally. Not surprisingly, these limousine maxis are often the most beautiful of all.

To Daniel Forster, "The shame is that the boats are used so little. The deliveries ought to be the real races for maxi boats, but races like the Capetown to Rio, or the Transatlantic are vanishing rather than becoming more popular."

There is currently little danger of a modern 12 Meter yacht being underemployed.

For years the pressure around the America's Cup has been unending and now that the Cup has gone to Perth, it is worse. These big, heavy, deeprunning yachts are plowing the seas all around the world, looking for some new bit of "magic". From a distance they are stately, close aboard they are nothing but hard physical labor, while materially they are in a constant flux between maintenance and failure.

12 Meters are designed to an old rule (their name refers to "meter" as a term of measurement rather than a unit of measurement), so they average about sixty-five feet in length that splits the difference between the radical departures of ocean racers and the one-design discipline of the Olympic classes. They are raced with all the intensity of one-designs, however, while the cost of building, equipping, canvassing and maintaining them makes even the wealthiest maxi owner cringe. Add to this the cost of transportation around the world (the last Championships were in Sardinia, the next in West Australia) for boat and crew, plus housing and feeding a few dozen sailors, designers and technicians for a three year campaign and you can see what kind of obsession they represent.

The removal of the America's Cup from America has had one major effect on the racing: the inclusion of corporate sponsors and advertising in the funding equation. Now skippers like Dennis Conner or Harold Cudmore and sailing entrepreneurs like Gary Jobson, have to spend almost as much time chasing dollars as they used to spend sailing their yachts. An event that used to be a remarkable form of competitive madness has now become an important business and it remains to be seen whether the competitors will be able to stay the course over the three or four year period between matches.

Is the sport worth such big-time sponsorship? Look at Daniel Forster's last pictures, the late afternoon spinnaker takedown on VICTORY. The curve of the sail, the billows of the collapsing chute, the sun glowing through the jib and the man perched out on the bow as it rises to the wave, those are the beauties of America's Cup racing. The rest is just money.

THE 1987 AMERICA'S CUP

THE SARDINIAN 12-METER COMPETITION

The show that was put on at the 12-Meter World Championships in Porto Cervo, Sardinia during the summer of 1984 heralded new directions for the style and substance of 12-Meter competition. No one may be able to match either the style or the substance of the Italians, but a lot of people will be trying between now and the Cup matches in Perth, Australia, in February 1987.

There have been attempts at a "world championship" in the Cup class before, most recently in England prior to the 1980 Cup match. These off-year meetings, under whatever name, have been uniformly uninspiring (the through-the-harbor start in the Xerox Cup in 1982 at Newport being a notable exception) because of the segregation maintained by the New York Yacht Club between good American boats and good foreign boats. In contrast, the Sardinian races were in fact legitimate championships, and then some, with a heavy undertone of "things to come" rumbling beneath the flourish of bigboat racing. The Twelves on hand ranged from the perennial, as in Gordon Ingates's GRETEL II, to the recently successful, as in Freedom, and included the proven competitive, AZZURRA, VICTORY '83, CHALLENGE 12, and CANADA 1. ENTERPRISE and FRANCE 3, two "never-quite-weres," rounded out the field. The event was broken into fleet and match-race championships, with most of the international interest in the fleet event, since it had the most potential for revealing the real and imagined speeds of the boats involved. There was a superabundance of style, a wealth of drama, sufficient hand wringing for Puccini, and enough opera buffa to remind an observer that the event was taking place in Italy. Discounting the event's unnerving portents, the Porto Cervians and the Aga Khan put on an excellent show.

On the up side there was a week and a half of very exciting fleet racing among eight 12-Meters, representing five countries, something unheard of while the New York Yacht Club and the American defense syndicates were calling the shots. The field was not exactly state of the art, nor were all the boats up to Cup form in terms of preparation and equipment, but the ones that were good were very, very good, and the ones that were not were colorful. The facilities at Porto Cervo were amazing. In place of the haphazard waterfront evolution of Newport, Porto Cervo boasted eight side-by-side hoists at the Centro del 12-Metrico, giving the place the appearance of an age-of-sail U-boat pen. Containers and trailers were stacked on the narrow foreshore, turning the scene into a kind of carnival rather than the armed camp delusion that so often was Newport. The wind generally cooperated with the racers, particularly those on the insides of the lifts, and currents were predictable. There were only two mistrals and one rainstorm, and the hospitality was lavish.

There were some anomalies; rival 12-Meter helmsmen Dennis Conner and John Kilius were, at different times, guest conductors aboard FREEDOM. The 1980 defender was racing under Italian colors but with U.S. sail numbers. Four of Alan Bond's minions sailed on CHALLENGE 12, of the Yacht Club de Carrara, and the Italian boat managed to be extremely slow when Dennis Conner was in town and extremely fast after he left. Buddy Melges and Bobby Mosbacher raced for the United States aboard a ragged French boat with a polyglot crew, but managed to win the panache award for the Midwest by sailing FRANCE 3 out of the tiny harbor under spinnaker each morning. Most amazing of all, AZZURRA, the Yacht Club Costa Smeralda boat, didn't win. This was about the only bit of style and substance that didn't fit the script in Porto Cervo.

On the race course, where the action was scheduled to take place, three boats showed that they had lots of speed on the fleet at different times. AZZURRA, CANADA 1, and CHALLENGE 12 each had a day in the limelight, sailing higher and faster than everyone else, but none of them won the regatta. Mauro Pelaschier sailed AZZURRA away from the fleet, in an apparent fit of pique, took a sixth in one race; the Azzurrans never made up the points. Terry MacLaughlin suffered the dismal fate of a destroyed headsail, as well as conditions that were usually a little too light for his ride. John Savage couldn't seem to find the fast lane until he got the worst start in the fleet in the last race. He then took CHALLENGE to the front in that race.

VICTORY '83, or Vittoria if you like, was the winner because she sailed an almost flawless series. She never had boatspeed on the fleet, although she was never out of the hunt, and she didn't make any stupid mistakes. Her Italian afterguard of Flavio Scala and Lorenzo Bortolotti was augmented by Rod Davis, designated helmsman for the EAGLE syndicate of the Newport Harbor (California) Yacht Club. They sailed out from under cover, protected their place in the standings, and didn't take flyers. Not taking flyers and remembering that the event wasn't a multiple match race assured their success.

Most of the foreign heavy-hitters left the Costa Smeralda after the 12-Meter meeting and the conclusion of the fleet racing. Everyone had his lessons to ruminate on. Syndicate managers will worry over funding, designers will fret over lines and skippers over schedules, and marketing men will ponder the "great licensing opportunities".

The consensus in the United States is that the Cup cannot be won without corporate sponsorship (Len Green and COURAGEOUS II notwithstanding), and every Yank in Sardinia was looking to see how the locals did it. In terms of corporate participation, the Italians are light years ahead of the rest of the world. In five years they have converted a previously unknown event into something like a national mania. In addition to AZZURRA's Who's Who of Italian Industry syndicate, two more Italian groups have formed to go to Australia. One of them is already funded to the point of surplus by a consortium as high powered as the one that came to Newport in 1983.

MEANWHILE BACK AT PERTH

The Royal Perth Yacht Club inherited both the prize and the problems of the New York Yacht Club, the previous defender, and like the New York Yacht Club in days of yore, it is already at the center of an uproar. By selling the rights to the Cup name in return for financial assistance to the club, it has siphoned off some prime syndicate sponsors, or so complain the people trying to fund Cup defenders. The scramble for spectator boats, broadcast rights, and "exclusives" puts the club in apparent conflict with at least one potential defender a day. One defense personality claims the Royal Perth is "doing all it can to keep us from successfully defending the Cup."

The local 12-Meter syndicates are already locked in combat over press, crew, facilities, and money, with Alan Bond's AUSTRALIA III effort slightly ahead. His AUSTRALIA II was beautifully resored in late 1984, and with her, Bondy's team can claim the only proven "state-of-the-art 12-Meter" in the world. Through January and February 1985, they tuned both the boat and her new crew in their own Indian Ocean. Better Fremantle than Newport, but the magnitude of their responsibility is just dawning on the Aussies. Skip Lissiman, former trimmer and now the beach boss of the group, speaks for most when he says that they "had no idea how much more important the Cup would become once we won it. There's no way to compare the time and money spent defending it to the effort we put into winning it in the first place. It means so much more now."

The Bond group has semipalacial headquarters on the commercial harbor, just a derisive hoot away from the New York Yacht Club compound. Project manager John Longley can look out his tinted windows at the shape of AMERICA II in her giant shed, cock an ear, shake his head, and declare that "they're changing keels again." Longley's boys are still going through the hamburger-helper part of the program, changing hands every day rather than keels. "New guys" are sea-trialed every week to find out which ones have the skills, interest, and personalities to make good match-race crew. After four runs at the Cup, there are some graying vets in the Bond camp, and the search for new bodies is as timely as the search for a new boat.

In a revisitation of the 1983 campaign, Bond has allied himself with another Australian team to produce semi-joint efforts. This time the South Australians, led by Sir James "Police Car" Hardy, have purchased a Ben Lexcen design from Bond. The new boat was built in Steve Ward's boatshop (another shrine on the 12-Meter pilgrimage), where AUSTRALIA III was also taking shape. The "crow eaters," as South Australians are affectionately nicknamed by their countrymen, were also allowed to sail AUSTRALIA II on alternate weekends in order to get a crew more or less ready for their yacht. The new boat then began sailing against AUSTRALIA II in a shakedown series that also served as full-size tank testing before the final touches were put on AUSTRALIA III. Lexcen describes the South Australians as "our fetus." "They are growing right out of our program," he adds, "and they'll get all our expertise from the very beginning. When they grow up, we'll get to use them."

A short way up the Swan River from the commercial harbor at Fremantle another homegrown effort is well under way. At the Task Force 1987 headquarters, Iain Murray (former helmsman of the 12-Meter ADVANCE and Australian 18 intergalactic champion) and designer John Swarbrick are putting the final touches on their new Twelve, largely financed by Perth businessman Kevin Parry. Parry's center is more like an insurance company than a 12-Meter syndicate, since he has, from the beginning, styled his program as far off the lines of Bond's as possible. At Task Force 1987 the plan all along has been to build two boats, sail them against each other, make them faster, and then win. Murray has stated that his non-Lexcen effort is good insurance against a "single-train-of-thought" disaster, but he and Swarbrick have by their own admission borrowed heavily from Lexcen's AUSTRALIA II, using models, photos, published drawings, and the like, and then modified the concept to fit their ideas of faster.

"The Americans" are very visible on the wind-blasted foreshore at the entrance to the commercial harbor. That is where the New York Yacht Club's AMERICA II syndicate has staked a three-year claim to one corner of Fremantle's largest and most professional industrial boatyard. Ensconced there is the New York Yacht Club's answer to hermit crab living: a 12-Meter campaign with all its technical trimmings designed around the shipping container. Art "Capt. Tuna" wullschleger, the beachmaster, runs herd on the container complex. There are containers for the machine shop, for rigging, for spares, for gear, and even containers for converting Auz power to U.S. power. The tarmac around the containers gets so hot in the late mornings (100 degrees Fahrenheit is not uncommon in midsummer) that the team laid down a patch of artificial tennis court for stacking sails, just so the bags don't stick to the ground. The instant nature of the facility extracts a psychic price, however. When the Fremantle doctor, as the steady afternoon breeze is called, whistles in, the rattles from the bare New York Yacht Club compound are deafening.

For all the outpost mentality, the New York Yacht Club organization may have stolen a march on the rest of the challengers, if only by figuring out how it is going to support several boats, a two crew team, and at least a few backers in 1987. It created its own real estate boomlet in Fremantle, taking up condos and a block of flats, and then it brought in its own logistics organization to make it work. By comparison, the Italians, who arrived to sail AZZURRA against AMERICA II, were barely camping out. The good old boys of the AMERICA II effort, O. L. Pitts and Lee Smith, of Forth Worth, New York, have gone as far as anyone could go toward making their effort at least semipopular in Western Australia, and the physical arrangement of the camp will be copied by everyone who can manage to fit that many containers onto his particular spot.

There were at least a few lessons learned by John Kolius, John Bertrand, and the rest of the New York Yacht Club crew. When asked if the trip to Perth was allowing the team to hone the edge of its program, one of the technical heavies in the AMERICA II camp responded, "Hone the edge? Hell, we don't even know what shape the knife shoud be yet." After a series of give-and-take "races" with AZZURRA, the team knows that it hasn't any spectacular breakthroughs with AMERICA II, but many seasoned observers are impressed with the Americans and their chances in 1987 — including AZZURRA's skipper, Cino Ricci.

ROBBY NAISH

Becoming a professional boardsailor was about the farthest thing from my mind when I first began windsurfing. Boardsailing wasn't baseball. There were no professionals, no money. The sport was heading off in the direction of sailboat racing, and even though I lived in Hawaii, where we had wind, surf and sunshine, the center of activity in the sport was on the other side of the world.

People were coming to Hawaii to shoot pictures of boardsailors, even in the early and mid-'70s. The backgrounds were exotic and beautiful, the conditions were far more challenging than those elsewhere.

We all started out racing in triangles on stock windsurfers. Then we moved out into the waves with those boards, but the boards did not work very well. By 1977 we began making custom boards which were basically faster windsurfer shapes, trying to make the boards fit the conditions. When I say "we" I mean a whole group of Kailua boardsailors, including Pat Love, Larry Stanley, Mike Horgan, my father Rick and many waves lovers.

The equipment really took off at the end of the '70s. In 1978 everyone realized that straps were the answer for staying attached to the board while in the air, in the surf and at high speed. At the same time board shapes and sail designs started changing radically. First we just cut off the backs of more or less standard shaped boards. Gradually boards became smaller and more refined, making them much more maneuverable for wave riding. By 1982 sailboards had progressed in design very much like scaled up surfboards. They got so small that uphauling the sail became pretty much obsolete, and waterstarting was the only answer. Nearly all the pictures in this book are of sailors on little boards.

Almost all of the advancements in the sport have been for the better with only a few exceptions. Since there is a great deal of money involved in the sport now, there is an undercurrent of competition, not always friendly competition. Most everyone is still out to have a good time, but you can sometimes sense tension at meets, especially among the younger sailors who have to get noticed in order to make a name for themselves.

Daniel Forster knows about the hustle. Many competitors have incentive clauses in their sponsorship contracts that pay them a bonus if their pictures appear in surfing magazines or calendars. I work for five sponsors, and I figure that my ability to get them publicity is the reason they pay me, so I don't have any incentive clauses. Also over the years I have started to think like a photographer. Now I know what the best time of the day is for shooting on a particular beach, and which are the best angles for the waves and the cameras.

By far the best part of the sport is the rapid evolution of equipment. The equipment we use today allows us to do things in the waves we never dreamed of five years ago. We used to get a new board every season, now we change board once a month.

I have heard that Daniel had no intention of becoming a sailing photographer, just like I had no idea that a person could make a living as a boardsailor. Windsurfing has been a dream come true for me, a sport full of opportunities. Daniel Forster has helped make it so.

GARY JOBSON

Sailing is for everyone, and Daniel Forster's photography proves it. Watching sailboats race is not like watching the grass grow as one writer once suggested. Forster's photographs offer action and competition by real people in the heat of battle giving everyone, veteran yachtsmen and beginners alike a new reason to go sailing. These photos put you into the game of sailing in a way no other pictures do.

Over the past decade I have presented over 700 slide lectures to groups ranging from school children to Yacht Clubs to corporate sales groups. Thanks to Daniel the spirit of sailing has been captured live. I wish you could have heard the cheers and enthusiasm generated by these audiences. In my slide talks to corporations the winning edge is the goal; Daniel's action photos demonstrate just what that edge is.

The spray frozen by the shutter makes Daniel's photography unique. His speciality is reflection, what the eye misses at the decisive moment is remembered by the camera.

Daniel's pictures capture the speed, the grace and the beauty of the sport. At the same time reveal the struggle and the intense competition. The individual faces, the teamwork, and the movement of people seem to come right out of his pictures. I look at thousands of slides every year, and it seems as though Daniel alone has the ability to capture the right moment exactly. His photos make sailing seem bigger than life.

Sailing has advanced rapidly over the past decade – composite high tech hulls, laminated sails, whiled keels are proof – and I think the sport will keep changing.

The current trend is toward higher-profile events, especially as more companies recognize the value of sailing for their own commercial ends.

When I sailed with Ted Turner on COURAGEOUS in 1977, sailors barely knew that the press existed. Turner changed all that, for the sailors and for the press. News magazines and network television carried stories about him, and through him they learned about sailing. Coincidentally, the first of many times I have had Daniel shooting on board was during that America's Cup campaign. Now, nine years, two America's Cups, a Fastnet disaster, and one Australia II later, the press is well aware that sailing exists and is an exciting, big-time sport.

The sport is evolving and one reason is that the public perception has changed. Portraits of massive yachts are giving way to close up pictures of events worth knowing about, events worth backing, worth remembering.

Most important, Daniel's photography allows sailors to appreciate their sport and attract new people to it.

DENNIS CONNER

Sailing is a sport with a fairly simple set of rules and conditions. It's a hobby, but given enough time and energy it can become a game of life. To excel requires a competitive spirit, dedication, motivation, leadership, drive, energy, cunning and at times especially when you lose, humility. If you approach sailing with total commitment, you will find that your hobby can establish standards that go well beyond the race course. The kind of effort you are willing to put forth and the integrity of your program will reflect the way you look at life.

Once you have set a goal, and established a level of commitment, strange things may begin to happen. If you attain your goals, your self-image improves. When you think of yourself as winner, your standards rise, and your successful performance becomes the norm. Your new goals are set on the assumption that you can do better. This can lead to a strange set of priorities, a kind of tunnel vision. When all your buddies are out cruising on the Fourth of July you might be on the dock working on something that you know isn't quite right. And that intense dedication fits in with your higher standards. Is it right to go out to the race course half-prepared? Is that fair to the designer and builder of your boat? Do you settle for second or third when you know in your heart that you could have been first? Someone would be cheated in that case, most likely the crew who sailed with you because they presumed you would put out your total effort. When you begin to play like a winner, and feel like a winner, others will start assuming you are a winner. Life's like that.

So what does all this have to do with Daniel Forster's photographs? I think Daniel is playing his game of life the way the best sailors he photographs do. Is he satisfied with the second best picture possible? I don't think so. When he is sent to some faraway sunny place by a magazine to shoot photographs of sailboats, does he do it from the bar? I don't think so. When he says that he will not be in the way on board a boat, does he immediately start giving stage directions and scattering his gear around? No. Will he work as hard at his job as the sailors he is photographing? Yes, without question. He is willing to spend days tracking down the Jim Kilroys of our sport in order to spend only minutes on the foredecks of the KIALOA IVs.

This makes Daniel unique. Over the years I have had thousands of cameras aimed at me, but I could count on one hand the photographers who really devote themselves to their craft, who show up at event after event, who actually know the boats and the people they are shooting. They are the ones who look at the sky and the surroundings the same way a good skipper does. They reach into their bags for a lens or a camera, the way a skipper calls for a new sail. They have to know what is needed, to be confident that it is the best one there is, and they have to use to its limits or beyond, because there won't be any second chances once the moment has passed. The Daniels of the world don't seem to be satisfied with just another picture. That's not how the game is played.

CINO RICCI

I have never passed Cape Horn, neither have I been to the Olympic games, but I have been sailing since I was a kid and have always had the sea in my blood.

I started to race during the sixties, in France and England. We raced there with spartan boats, which in Italy would have been inconceivable. I "imported" that kind of racing around 1969: empty boats, interiors with only the bare essentials, cloth berths, no comfort.

The America's Cup entered my life in 1981. Since childhood it had been a legend for me, and I knew all the names of the great helmsmen that had raced in it. However, when some important personalities of our sailing world came to me and talked about an Italian challenge, I was puzzled and hesitant; I did not think that we would be in a position to do the race justice, without any experience in 12-Meter racing.

Then I spoke about it with Tom Blackhaller, a close experienced friend since 1974. He convinced me. He told me that the America's Cup was a unique experience, that I could not let it escape, that I had to do it. The idea of starting such an enterprise frightened, but I agreed. We already had the designer, Vallicelli. We also had the right sparring partner. When we succeeded in convincing Gianni Agnelli to sponsor our entry we felt even more confident. Then the Aga Khan came in, and the operation took off.

In Newport with AZZURRA we ended third amongst the challengers. In the beginning I had not imagined such' a good result but apparently we learned fast. We Italians are improvisers and, besides, the close competition with so many challengers certainly forced us improve fast. We are now working for the second challenge. The aim is to do better, though this time it will be even more difficult. This time the Americans are challengers and I am still convinced that they are the strongest team, stronger even than the Australians.

Through my involvement in the America's Cup with AZZURRA, I have learned many things, among them the role of the press in sailing. When I raced for fun and I did not worry about them. Today sponsors carry a lot of power, and, logically enough, they want to have a return on their investment in terms of publicity and image. Thus the function of the press has become very important; particularly valued is fine photography.

For me a good yachting photographer has to be a good sailor. It is the only way he can forsee the right moment to take the right picture. Daniel Forster is a sailor. I would not take him on board if he was not a good sailor, at ease on the boat. Behind his lens Daniel feels the boat as a member of the crew. He senses a couple of seconds in advance what is going to happen and is ready to capture it on film at the right moment.

In my opinion Daniel succeeds because he takes part in the race, he is involved in it. Contrary to most others, he speaks the sailor's language, knows what to do, and constantly amazes us by distilling the essence of sailing action into images that never lose their appeal.

A C R O B A T I C

T

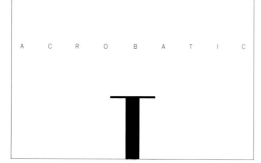

Hookipa Beach, Maui, Hawaii. This picture was taken in 1981 when I made my first trip to Hawaii. The windsurfers' equipment was very basic then. The boards were long, the sails were in light Dacron and the wishbones too long, which made the rig difficult to handle.

Two of today's stars in the waves: Peter Cabrinha on the yellow board he shaped himself and superstar Robby Naish on his legendary "star"-board. The shot was taken during one of the many competitions in Maui sponsored by the wetsuit manufacturer O'Neill. Forty of the world's best windsurfers are on the beach for a week making that bit of surf a photographer's dream. The sailors compete in elimination trials, two groups of two at a time in 8 minute heats. Peter won in the Fall of 1983 and Robby, for the first time after many attempts, in Spring 1984.

Jill Boyer, winner of the women's division, trying a waterstart in the Hookipa breakers.

A perfect "Head-dip".

Another member of the Naish family, Rick, Robby's father, at Birdshit-Rock, off Kailuha Bay on Oahu. The Rock became famous during the Pan Am Windsurfing contest. It was one of the marks the boardsailors had to round.

The record for the crossing from Maui to Molokai has been set by Robby many times. Baron Arnaud de Rosnay, the French windsurfer lost in 1984 between China and Formosa, founded this classic in 1981. Here Robby uses a long narrow board, made for long distances in one direction, called a "gun".

Jaap van der Rest from Holland, former world speed record holder, in Hawaiian waves.

A Pan Am windsurfing event in Kailuha Bay.

Rocks and currents are the main hazards in Hookipa. Everyone expects monster waves.

Frazer Black, originally from Great Britain, arrived in Hawaii when the sport started to take off and is now one of the few Europeans who has made it as a professional windsurfer.

An "aerial off-the-lip". Notice the muscular upper body these wave riders have.

"Off-the-lip" into the evening sun at Hookipa.

Mike Waltze takes off on a breaking wave. He actually landed the board flat on the water and sailed away!

An "off-the-lip" by Robby Naish. In the repertoire of every wave-jumping windsurfer, this manoeuvre involves sailing to the edge of a wave without losing speed and taking off much like a skier over a mogul.

Matt Schweitzer, the son of Hoyle Schweitzer who officially started it all, in the "washing machine".

Malte Simmer emmigrated from Germany to start his own sailloft. He is showing off a state-of-the-art sail, October 1984, in front of a "pipeline".

When Matt Schweitzer hits a big wave in Hookipa he jumps higher than anybody else.

Nobody shows more control while jumping than Robby Naish, shown here on his favorite "star"-board. This picture was taken with a 500 mm lens and an extenders (2 x).

Rhonda Smith, president of the Professional Women's Board-sailing Association, in typical Hookipa conditions.

It can be wild in Hookipa, especially when big breaking waves, surfers, bodysurfers and windsurfers meet. But the old rule is still valid: surfers have priority over windsurfers.

Diamond Head, Oahu, Hawaii. I headed out to swim in the surf with my waterproof camera but before I reached the waves this lonely windsurfer reached for the beach.

Mike Waltze, Maui's hero does a bottom-turn one late evening during the O'Neill Contest in Hookipa.

Randy Naish is the wildest member of the Naish family; every wave is afraid to be slashed by him. When we flew over him with the helicopter he tried to land right in our cockpit.

For lots of jumpers the take-off is the easy part, it's the landing that's the problem.

Mark Angulo, son of Ed Angulo, the famous board shaper, is one of the newcomers to watch. He surfed in the big Hookipa waves when he was fourteen and in 1985, at 16, made it into the top three! This picture was taken with the new CANON 1,200/5.6 lens. This marvel of optical engineering cannot be bought, only borrowed. As you can see in this photograph, clean colors and extraordinary sharpness are proof of its technological superiority.

Randy Naish, Robby's younger brother, introduced the "star"-board and the "star"-sail seen in a previous picture: it is now the family trademark.

This photograph of Mike Waltze falling of his board with Robby Naish sailing by was the Sports Category winner of the 25th World Press Photo Contest 1982.

It was late in the afternoon at Hookipa beach, just barely enough light to use the 500 mm lens with an extender (1.4 x), during the final of the O'Neill contest. Suddenly Robby jumped and Matt Schweitzer sailed by. When their trajectories crossed it looked like Matt's mast would pierce Robby!

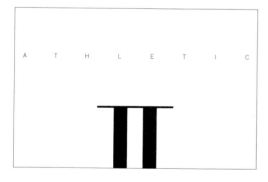

Take one wave out of nowhere and two board sailors and you have an interesting study of jumping styles. Matt Schweitzer gets the perfect angle while Mark Paul from Australia takes off a little too early. After an attempted "donkey-kick" Paul lands in full control, while Matt just keeps flying and flying...

Shooting from the right side of Hookipa one day I looked over towards the mountains near Kahului. This picture of three airborne windsurfers is a shot that won't be forgotten and, when I saw it through my lens, I yodeled.

A T H L E T I C

FINN

John Bertrand, silver medal winner Los Angeles Olympic Games 1984. After a long battle on the race course and in the courthouses he finally made the US selections to race in Long Beach. He thanked the people who stood behind him with a silver medal.

Kiel Week, leeward mark after 2nd reach.

FLYING DUTCHMAN

Going for the start. Olympic since 1960, built in 1951 by the Dutchman U. van Essen, this dinghy is the fastest monohull in the Olympic classes. It is one of the few international classes where wooden hulls are as competitive as glass fiber hulls, but Kevlar fibers have allready been used for at least one hull...

"Finnsailors are sturdy individualists. They prefer to sail and race alone for then they know that they will have nobody else to blame but themselves. For such people, the Finn dinghy which has been in the Olympics since 1952, has special appeal. There are faster, lighter, more modern singlehanders than the Finn but none better for sorting the men from the boys. The Finn turns quickly for really tactical racing yet that big sail of well over a hundred and ten square feet with its eleven foot mainboom has turned the muscles of many a fit strong young man into soft rubber." Thats how the late Jack Knights, eminent Yachting journalist, sees this dinghy.

Ski Yachting Cannes, France. Former Worldchampion, Germans Schwarz-Fröschl, show their style.

An Austrian crew slices through the Baltic spray during Kiel Week, the biggest race week in the world with over 1,200 boats racing!

Los Angeles Olympics 1984. Jonathan McKee and William Carl Buchan bring the gold medal home. The same day William's father won gold in the Star class! But the American team broke another record: they won gold or silver medals in all seven Olympic classes racing in Long Beach.

Terry McLaughlin and Evert Bastet, Canada, going for the silver in Long Beach.

470

The 470 joined the ranks of the Olympic classes in 1976. A "one-design", as are all the other six Olympic sailing classes, each detail of the boat's construction must conform to the rules governing the class, and is overseen by the International Yacht Racing Union. Sails, mast, boom and the boat's 470 centimeter overall length are identical on each boat, as designated in the original French designed plans. Now the most popular Olympic dinghy, the 470 attracts the most athletic sailors and, some say, the wildest.

Ski Yachting in Cannes. Different approaches to the jibing mark in Mistral conditions. The Italian helmsman on the inside boat lets everything go and hopes for the best.

Kiel Week, the windward mark. Because of strict one design rules, the 470s are very close in speed and you often see big pile-ups at the first mark.

Jibing with women crew. In 1985 the International Yacht Racing Union decided to create a separate class for women. The 470 Olympic Women Class was born.

1984 Olympics Long Beach. The Canadian crew tries to cut through at the first mark.

The Hunger brothers from Germany enjoying a victory in Long Beach. They finished fourth overall, a most unfortunate placing in the Olympics where one remembers only the first three.

TORNADO

The Swiss crew of Rolf Zwicky and Christoph Brüllmann enjoy a wild ride on the way home from Olympic racing in Long Beach.

Kiel Week. Tasting the spray!

Rex Sellers and Christopher Timms finished in the top three in all the six races in the 84 Olympics and did not have to sail the last one to win a gold medal! With another gold medal in the Finn class the New Zealand team was second in Long Beach.

Kiel Week excitement.

The Brazilian crew at the Olympics in 1984.

The Tornado became one of the Olympic classes in 1976 in Kingston, Ontario, part of the Montreal Olympic Games the same year. One sees in the photograph why this catamaran is called a "flying platform". This fastest of all the seven one-design classes participating in the Games can attain speeds in excess of twenty knots.

No collection of photographs of the Olympic sailing classes would be complete without a photograph of Poul Elvström. Nobody else has ever won four Olympic gold medals in a row and from 1948 till 1960 he was the best singlehanded dinghy sailor in the world. He went on to win the 1966 Star World Championship, to mention one of many more.
In this photograph, Poul is racing with his youngest daughter Trine in Long Beach. They missed the bronze medal by 0.7 points!

STAR

The Star was designed in 1910 by New Yorker Francis Sweis-guth and became Olympic class in 1932. The design has not changed much since then and the class is still as popular as ever.
In this Los Angeles 1984 Olympics start picture, notice the ma-jor caracteristic of the Star which is also its vulnerable point: the long, slender mast.

A jibbing sequence on a Star is like a "pas-de-deux" for two athletes where the slightest fault means losing the whole rig.

P O W E R F U L

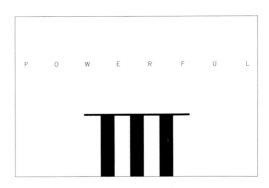

I even met a crew member who enjoys racing!

SOLING

The Soling, a three-person boat with a keel, first competed in Kiel in 1972, as part of the Munich Olympics. The special feature of this almost 27 foot (8.15 meter) boat is a self tacking jib. Here in Kiel, the crews gybe at the mark.

This helicopter photograph shows three maxi boats at the start of the Boca Grande Race sailing under the St. Petersburg Bay bridge. KIALOA leads WINDWARD PASSAGE and BUMBLEBEE. One foggy night a tanker ran into the northbound traffic side of the bridge and the whole middle section collapsed. It hasn't been rebuilt yet and makes a photograph you have to look twice at.

Gary Jobson, tactician of the two-time America's Cup winner COURAGEOUS steers MIDNIGHT SUN out of St. Petersburg Bay.

At the start of the Ocean Triangle a bird's-eye view of the crystal clear water.

The fleet approaches the windward mark and the crews prepare to hoist the spinnakers. The Norwegian crew (with the standing crewmember) eventually lost the silver medal in the last race. Suffering a disqualification for pumping, they finished fifth.

Alain Testuz and his crew from Switzerland on a hard reaching leg in Kiel.

Rod Davis prepares to gybe while crewmember Edward Trevelyan thoroughly enjoys the sail because these Americans appear to be far ahead of the rest of the fleet. Robby Haines and his crew went on to capture the gold.

During each spinnaker take-down there are a few moments when the kite is being gathered up on deck and it billows and rolls in the breeze. Being in the right position when this is happening is very rewarding photography. This shot of INSANITY is one of my favorite photographs.

For several years in a row the yacht WILLIWAW arrived at the start of the first race looking brand new. The game was to find out if this was just a superb paint job or if it was actually a new boat that year. Dennis Conner (in white T-shirt) is at the helm.

Lowell North's crew trims the spinnaker during the Nassau Cup on SLEEPER.

An exciting Nassau Cup start with 22 knots of wind and short, steep waves. At least the Bahamian spray was warm.

Almost ten years of sailing as a team paid off for the American Soling goldmedalists. After the sixth race Haines, Trevelyan and Davis had such a wide margin between themselves and the rest of the fleet that it was unnecessary to sail the seventh race.

OBSESSION, a custom 46 foot design by the well-known Sparkman & Stephens design office was one of the first I.O.R. boats with the characteristic S&S stern. This photograph was taken in 1978 but the 1980 America's Cup winner FREEDOM also has a similar stern.

ADMIRAL'S CUP

The Admiral's Cup still claims to be the unofficial world championship of offshore yachts. More countries build new yachts for the selection trials than for any other event. Based in Cowes on the Isle of Wight the racing was formerly held almost exclusively on the Solent. The English conceded, however by changing the location of some of the races, that racing around the Solent's mudbanks and in its tides was not always fair to foreign teams.
The schedule of racing is currently two short races called "Solent triangles", the 220 mile Channel Race and an Olympic triangle in Christchurch Bay. The final race, the famous Fastnet, starts in Cowes, goes to the lighthouse south of Ireland and back to Plymouth, a 607 mile long haul.

The Swiss yacht NADIA takes a chance on port tack start. The skipper Jürg Christen tacked a few seconds later and was ahead of the fleet.

(SORC) SOUTHERN OCEAN RACING CONFERENCE

This first series of the season starts in February in St. Petersburg, Florida with a 135 mile race to Boca Grande and back, then a 370 mile race bringing the fleet around Key West to Fort Lauderdale. Out of Miami the 60 participating yachts sail a 35 mile and a 135 mile triangle, the latter called the Ocean Triangle to Fort Lauderdale, Ocean Cay, Bahamas and back to Miami. The Miami to Nassau race, 172 miles, is followed by the final race in the series, the Nassau Cup.

After five races of boring weather this 1985 Nassau Cup start had 22 knots of wind and the sky was cloudless. Everyone looks forward to this race because the water and air are warm and clear.

The TOGO crew has just rounded the downwind mark and is trying to reef the mainsail. A Japanese team competed in Cowes for the second time in 1983.

The Australian yacht POLICE CAR, owned by Sir James Hardy of the vineyard-owning family, sails along the Cowes waterfront and over the Royal Yacht Squadron finishing line.

When racing in the Solent you are usually trying to avoid a strong countercurrent while at the same time trying to avoid running aground. If you don't check the tide charts carefully you could find yourself sailing backward. The Japanese yacht MIYAKODORI III is trying to translate the shouting "starboard" and avoid a collision as well.

Typical Solent light on the American entry SCARAMOUCHE and SUPERSTAR of Melbourne.

The fleet reaches down the Solent towards the English channel. The boats in the foreground have just seen the yachts ahead of them get a fresh breeze and are rapidly taking down their spinnakers, while the yachts at the back of the fleet haven't yet noticed the new wind. They are in for a surprise.

The Italian yacht BRAVA faces an English sky. The Admiral's Cup is unique in its photographic conditions. The water has a strong greenish cast and the sky is extremely changeable. This dark blue wall threatening rain is a common Solent sight.

A perfect broaching sequence thanks to the Dutch boat FOR-MIDABLE (former MARIONETTE). After a few leeward-windward rock and rolls the helmsman lost control and the spinnaker took over. The huge sail area of the spinnaker pulled the yacht over and the crew waited sitting on the rail in the water for the release of the vang. Finally the boom swept over the deck (sequence 4 and 5), the spinnaker sheet was released and the weighted keel (55% of the boat's total weight is in the lead) won over the wind.

CLIPPER CUP

The Pan Am Clipper Cup, based in Honolulu, is a yachtsman's dream. The 20-25 knot tradewinds and constant sunshine accompany the fleet for the three Olympic triangles, a 120 mile race to Molokai and back and a 720 mile race around the state of Hawaii. The three boat teams represent Hong Kong, New Zealand, Australia, Japan and the United States.

A view of the entire fleet approaching Honolulu.

The Japanese yacht SUPERWITCH and the American IRRATIO-NAL surf on the Pacific swell. IRRATIONAL is hitching a ride on SUPERWITCH's quarter wave, a technique introduced on the international offshore scene back in 1978 by Dennis Conner.

The Clipper Cup series is often called "the demolition derby" because of the amount of damage the boats incur during the course of the five races. BAD HABITS from New Zealand and SUNBIRD from Japan (J1710) demonstrate this at the reaching mark.

An interesting spinnaker take-down by Tom Blackaller's crew on BULLFROG, at the leeward mark the trimmer lets the after-guy go and the crew gets the spinnaker ready with the take-down line fixed in the middle of the spi. With this method the boom does not have to be lowered and the kite can be flown right up the mark.

The French yacht ENTREPRISE powerslides around the mark seen reflected in the hull. The crew is fully occupied in sheeting in the main jib, saving the spinnaker and lowering the spinnaker boom.

NUOVA of Italy engaged in the same manoeuvre as the previous picture but from a different angle.

The crew on board British team member PANDA is looking in every direction but at the spinnaker which will soon be completely in the water.

SCHTROUMPF from France appears to manage their spinnaker take-down with only one crewman.

A helicopter photograph offers a bird's eye view of a spinnaker take-down. The competition on the racing circuit is so stiff that there are many new manoeuvres that sailors have developed to have an edge over their opponents. In this photograph of GLORY (on the right) and SWIFTSURE the spinnakers are flown until the very last second instead of being taken down before the mark. At the top of the rounding mark, with the jib already fully taken in, the halyard is released. The crew then wrestles with the thousands of square feet of Dacron while the yacht beats to windward.

SOUTHERN CROSS SERIES

The Australian summer is the setting for this final series of the racing year, with the races running from before Christmas until New Year's Eve in Tasmania. Three triangle races and a middle distance race up the east coast north of Sydney and back are usually run in very hot weather. The series ends with the Sydney-Hobart Race, 630 miles on the open sea.

VENGEANCE (the former SISKA) heads toward Hobart during the 1983 Sydney-Hobart Race. Behind her is another maxi boat GIB AN INCH (formerly HELSAL II). The Sydney-Hobart is open to any I.O.R. boat as well as the Southern Cross boats.

A member of the Hong Kong team THE FRUMIOUS BANDERSNATCH (the owner is a Lewis Carroll fan) with Sydney's North Head in the background.

SARDINIA CUP

Held every two years alternating with the Admiral's Cup, the Sardinia Cup is the highlight of the Mediterranean racing season. From Porto Cervo (Sardinia, Italy) the boats compete in three triangles, a middle distance race to Asinara (Sardinia) and a long distance race to Hyères (France) and back.

Sailing in Sardinia means facing either very light wind or a very strong Mistral on a bottomless emerald blue sea 70 degrees Fahrenheit warm. No one minds how hard it blows because there is always a delicious plate of pasta waiting back on shore.

BANDIDO BANDIDO, a Hong Kong entry in 1983, goes to windward. The yacht and crew were easy to spot at sea and in the harbour because of their trademark "bandit" on the mainsail, hull and crew T-shirts.

NUOVA of Italy and COYOTE of France on their way to Hyères for the long distance race. The wind-eroded cliffs form a dramatic backdrop for these beautiful racing yachts.

Spinnaker take-down during a triangle race. The kite isn't in the water, it's just hidden by the Pacific swell.

An unusual photograph because it contains all three boats of the 1984 Sardinia Cup wining team. The German trio is led by CONTAINER, who is followed by PINTA (with the green spinnaker) and RUBIN (G33).

The Dutch crew on FORMIDABLE with Steve Bakker at the helm gybs close on the mark and then suddenly sees that the French yacht is trying to pass inside.

This is a good example of the telescoping effect of a long, in this case 400 mm, lens. TAURUS II, part of the Tasmanian team, appears to be bearing down on my motorboat. The yacht is approaching the gybing mark and the crew is ready to explode into activity. The actual distance between TAURUS II and me is several meters and I am on the other side of the mark.

About forty miles from the finish of the Sydney-Hobart Race the boats must round the southern end of Tasman Island. I waited here, at the mouth of Derwent River, hoping the boats would arrive before sunset to take this photograph with breath-taking "organ pipes" in the background. ZERO, a Japanese entry, obliged, and we followed her for about thirty minutes in the failing light until I was happy with the shot.

PRESTIGIOUS

IV

KIALOA IV dramatically changed yacht racing at the upper level of the International Offshore Rule (I.O.R.). By designing a yacht to the upper limit of the rule – a 70 foot rating with a hull measuring 81 feet – Ron Holland made Jim Kilroy the first owner of a real "maxi boat" and precipitated the commission of a number of other Class A boats. Racing with a crew of 26 including a full-time cook, the yachts are organised like a small business. KIALOA IV was the oldest maxi in Newport in June 1985, all of four years old, and Kilroy was about to begin construction of KIALOA V. KIALOA IV is shown here just after her launching in Florida in the 1981 SORC in St. Petersburg.

KIALOA IV showing her keel in the 1981 Maxi Week in Cowes. A typical maxi year includes racing in Florida, Antigua, Newport, Rhode Island, Palma di Mallorca, Porto Cervo, St. Tropez and possibly the Sydney-Hobart Race.

Rounding the forts at the entrance to the Solent, KIALOA IV gives an idea of the height of her mast.

A helicopter photograph showing a maxi's speed while close reaching. Even without a spinnaker KIALOA is probably doing 12-13 knots crashing through this wave on her way to Fort Lauderdale.